TOAD OVERLOAD

With warm thanks to the Columbus
Zoo, and especially to Barbara Ray
and Jack the toad.

Library of Congress Cataloging-in-Publication Data
Toad overload : a true tale of nature knocked off balance in
Australia / by Patricia Seibert : illustrated by Jan Davey Ellis.
p. cm.
Summary: Explains what happened when giant toads were
brought to Australia to help control beetles that ate the sugar
cane crop. Includes information on the physical characteristics
and habits of this species of toads.
ISBN 1-56294-613-7 (lib. bdg.)
1. Bufo marinus—Australia—Juvenile literature. 2. Pest
introduction—Environmental aspects—Australia—Juvenile
literature. 3. Sugarcane—Diseases and pests—Biological control—
Environmental aspects—Australia—Juvenile literature. [1. Giant
toad. 2.Toads. 3. Animal introduction—Australia. 4. Pests.] I. Ellis,
Jan Davey, ill. II. Title.
SB998.B82S45   1995
597.8'7—dc20   95-14179   CIP   AC

Published by The Millbrook Press
2 Old New Milford Road, Brookfield, Connecticut 06804

TOAD OVERLOAD

A TRUE TALE OF NATURE KNOCKED OFF BALANCE IN AUSTRALIA

BY PATRICIA SEIBERT

ILLUSTRATED BY JAN DAVEY ELLIS

The Millbrook Press
Brookfield, Connecticut

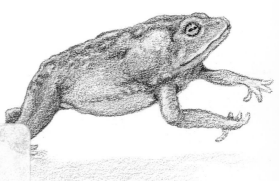

First there were 101. Now there are millions. They were supposed to be a solution to a problem. Now they *are* a problem. What are they? Very big toads. What happened? Here is the strange story.

Back in the early 1900s in Australia, farmers who grew sugarcane were facing some big problems. Beetles loved eating the leaves of sugarcane plants. Beetle babies, called grubs, loved eating the roots.

The Australian sugarcane growers were angry. They wanted to stop the beetles and nothing they tried was working.

In some other places around the world, sugarcane growers had been fighting off beetles and grubs, too. Scientists and growers had found a weapon that they thought might work—big, fat, hungry toads that loved to eat insects.

How big were the toads? As big as dinner plates.

Full grown, these toads were 9 inches (23 centimeters) long and almost 7 inches (18 centimeters) wide. Some grew even bigger. In fact, this kind of toad is one of the biggest toads on earth.

These big toads are known by several names, including giant toad and marine toad. When people decided to put the toads into sugarcane fields to eat insect pests, a new name came into use—cane toad.

Originally, the toads only lived in Central and South America, where it is wet and warm. Warm, wet weather is the kind the toads like best.

Back in the early 1900s in Australia, farmers who grew sugarcane were facing some big problems. Beetles loved eating the leaves of sugarcane plants. Beetle babies, called grubs, loved eating the roots.

The Australian sugarcane growers were angry. They wanted to stop the beetles and nothing they tried was working.

In some other places around the world, sugarcane growers had been fighting off beetles and grubs, too. Scientists and growers had found a weapon that they thought might work—big, fat, hungry toads that loved to eat insects.

How big were the toads? As big as dinner plates.

Full grown, these toads were 9 inches (23 centimeters) long and almost 7 inches (18 centimeters) wide. Some grew even bigger. In fact, this kind of toad is one of the biggest toads on earth.

These big toads are known by several names, including giant toad and marine toad. When people decided to put the toads into sugarcane fields to eat insect pests, a new name came into use—cane toad.

Originally, the toads only lived in Central and South America, where it is wet and warm. Warm, wet weather is the kind the toads like best.

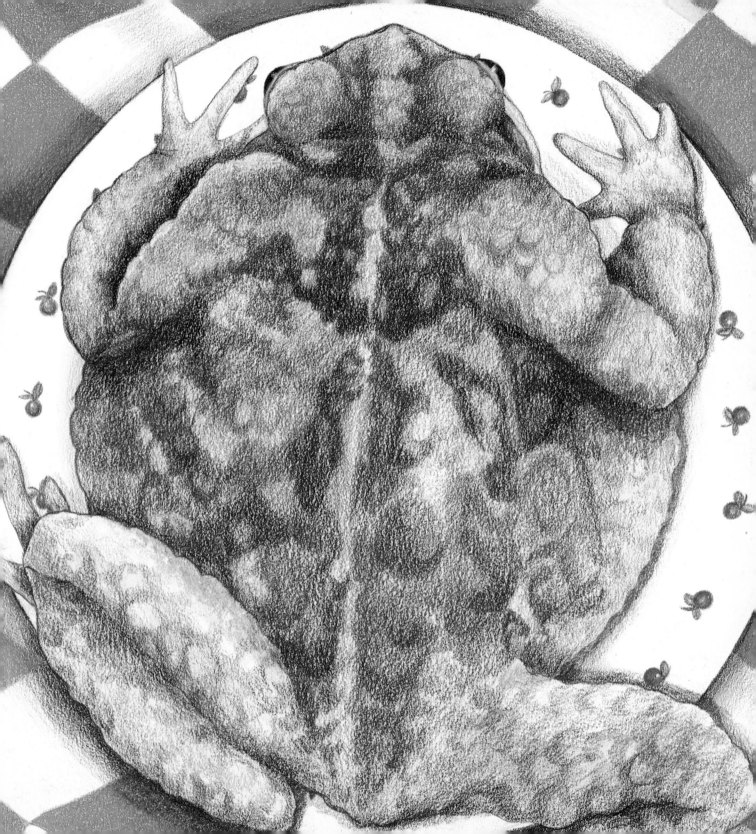

Some scientists and growers decided to put these giant toads with the giant appetites into the Australian sugarcane fields. The plan was for the toads to eat lots and lots of beetles.

In 1935, 102 toads were packed into crates and shipped to Australia. One died on the trip, but the 101 survivors were put into a pond in northeast Australia.

Would they live? Yes. The first 101 toads lived. Before too long, the females laid long, necklace-like strings of eggs. Each string contained thousands of tiny eggs.

The eggs hatched. The pond was filled with squirming, wriggling tadpoles.

The tadpoles grew into toadlets—baby toads. Then the toadlets were taken to cane fields and turned loose.

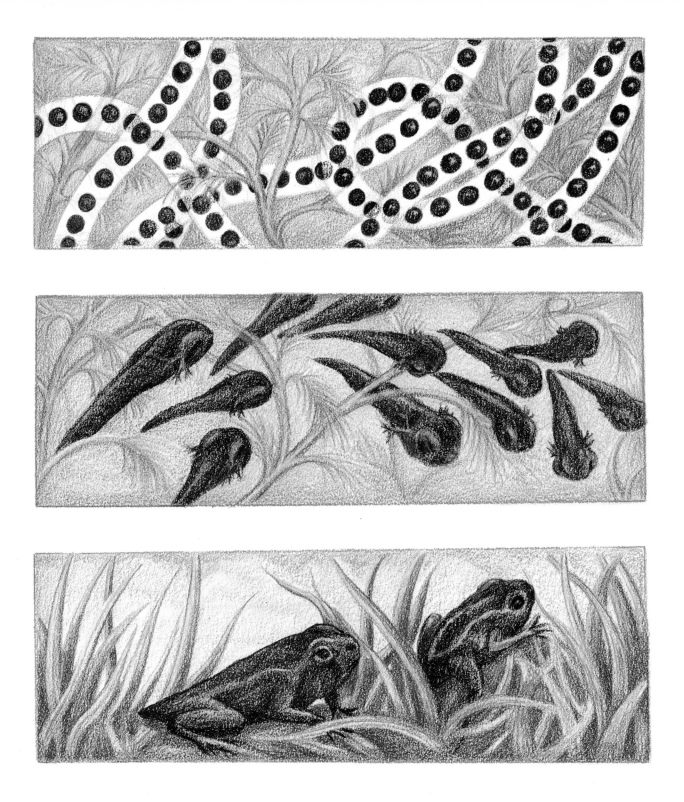

Would these newcomers eat the sugarcane pests, as they were brought to Australia to do? Yes and no. Some of the toads did eat some of the beetles and beetle grubs. But it was work for the toads to try and catch the beetles, which could fly away.

Also, the toads like to rest during the day and eat all night. The Australian cane fields were too sunny and dry. The toads like to snooze where it is shady and wet.

Soon, the toads found their way from field to town. The townspeople's lush gardens and watered lawns were very inviting.

The toads were much happier in town, where it was easy to find a satisfying meal. At night, in the circles of light shed by the lampposts, toads gathered. With almost no effort at all, they could gulp down the bugs that dropped to the ground after coming too close to the light.

Dazed bugs were not the only easy meals that the toads found. They also enjoyed eating from bowls of food left outside for pet dogs and cats.

It was a disappointment, of course, that the toads did not bother much with the grubs and beetles . But the real problem with the toads was something else—as time passed, more and more toads were appearing.

In Queensland, the state in Australia where the toads were first released, they could be found EVERYWHERE. They were all over the lawns and all through the gardens.

They slept under flowerpots and
inside boots left on back porches.
Sometimes the roads were covered with
toads—which was a very dangerous
situation for the toads.

For most people, the giant toads were a giant nuisance. A few people, however, liked the big-eyed creatures with the bumpy, brownish skin. Some people treated the toads like pets, actually letting them come inside their homes. Some children dressed the toads up like dolls!

Not everyone agrees that handling the toads is a good idea. These giant toads are poisonous.

If a toad is squeezed too hard, or if another animal tries to bite a toad—*watch out!* Poison squirts out several feet into the air, or into the mouth of whatever is biting the toad.

Usually, Australian animals die if they try to eat the toxic toads.

Australia seems to be an ideal home for the toads. They are not killed off by any diseases. They find plenty to eat. When it comes to laying eggs, a mud puddle will do. Millions and millions of toads are living where once there were none.

Are the toads causing bad problems in Australia? Scientists are trying to find out.

Meanwhile, many Australians have already decided that there are too many toads. Near the city of Brisbane, a "toad roundup" is held every year. People try to catch as many toads as possible.

As this strange story shows, when a plant or an animal is moved to a new habitat, no one can know for sure *what* might happen. The people who brought the toads to Australia hoped that after a while most of the beetles would be gone. Instead, before too many years had passed, there were giant toads everywhere.

Once those big toads came, they conquered!

Well ... almost.

MORE ABOUT
AUSTRALIA'S CANE TOADS

WHAT IS THE SCIENTIFIC NAME OF THE CANE TOAD?

Bufo marinus (Boo-foe muh-reen-us). *Bufo* means "toad." In addition to being called "cane toads," these toads are also called marine toads, giant toads, giant American toads, and Mexican toads.

The word *marinus* means "of (or pertaining to) the sea," but these toads do not make their homes in salt water. They often live near a coast, however, and the tadpoles will grow in brackish water, which is slightly salty.

HOW MANY EGGS DOES A CANE TOAD LAY AT ONE TIME?

The female toad lays the eggs. She lays as many as 30,000 eggs at one time in a long string of clear, jelly-like material. The female toad always lays the eggs in a body of water—a pond, a stream, or even a mud puddle.

HOW LONG DOES IT TAKE TOAD EGGS TO GROW INTO TOADS?

After the eggs are laid, it takes a week or less before they hatch into tadpoles. The tadpoles take between one and two months to reach the toadlet—baby toad—stage. The toadlets are able to hop out of the pond and start living on land. After four or five months, they are full-size toads.

DO THE TOADS MAKE ANY SOUND?

Yes, they make a low, trilling sound. Some people say the sound is like the engine of a car or tractor off in the distance. Because there are so many toads in Australia, sometimes the sound can be quite loud.

WHERE DO THE TOADS STORE THEIR POISON?

The toads have two big pouch-like glands. These glands start behind their eyes and extend far down the sides of their bodies. The poison is inside the glands. It is a milky-looking liquid. The bigger the toad, the more poison there is.

Cane toad eggs and tadpoles are poisonous, too. The toadlet stage is the only time when the toads are not poisonous enough to cause illness or death to predators who eat them.

WHAT HAPPENED TO THE SUGARCANE CROPS WHEN THE TOADS DID NOT EAT THE BEETLES AND GRUBS THAT WERE DESTROYING THE CROPS?

A chemical was developed that killed the beetles. Sugarcane is still a major crop in Australia.

DO AUSTRALIANS HUNT THE TOADS AND USE THEM FOR ANY PURPOSE?

Yes, many toads are caught each year and shipped to schools and laboratories in Australia and many other countries. These toads are dissected. The toads are good subjects for dissection because their organs are easy to see. Over 100,000 cane toads are sold each year for purposes of dissection.

Also, cane toad skin is tanned to make leather. Belts and wallets and other goods are made from the leather.

DO THE TOADS IN THE ROADS EVER GET HIT BY CARS AND TRUCKS?

Yes, all the time. There is a popping sound as a toad is run over by a vehicle. And in areas where lots of toads have been run over, there is often a bad smell.

HOW MUCH OF AUSTRALIA HAVE THE TOADS MOVED INTO?

This map shows the location where the toads were first released in the country of Australia.

This map shows all the places where cane toads were living in Australia by the 1990s, just a little more than 50 years after the first 101 toads were put into the pond in northeast Australia.

ABOUT THE AUTHOR
AND ILLUSTRATOR

This is Patricia Seibert's second non-fiction picture book published by The Millbrook Press, her first being *Mush! Across Alaska in the World's Longest Sled-Dog Race* which was named a Notable Children's Trade Book in the Field of Social Studies by the National Council for the Social Studies and the Children's Book Council. Ms. Seibert lives in Columbus, Ohio, where she works for a publishing company.

Jan Davey Ellis's illustration credits include three books published by the Millbrook Press: *The Winter Solstice* by Ellen Jackson, *Mush! Across Alaska in the World's Longest Sled-Dog Race* by Patricia Seibert, and *Fiesta! Mexico's Great Celebrations* by Elizabeth Silverthorne. *Fiesta!*, as well as *Mush!*, was a Notable Children's Trade Book in the Field of Social Studies. *The Winter Solstice* was named a Children's Choice book by the International Reading Association/Children's Book Council. Ms. Ellis lives in Columbus, Ohio, where she paints wall murals.